curious about
PHOENIX

BY GINA KAMMER

AMICUS LEARNING

What are you

CHAPTER ONE

Phoenix Legends
PAGE
4

CHAPTER TWO

Phoenix Life
PAGE
10

curious about?

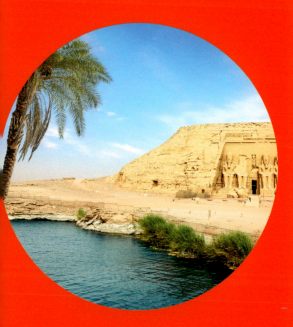

CHAPTER THREE

Finding Phoenix
PAGE **16**

Stay Curious! Learn More . . .22

Glossary. 24

Index 24

Curious About is published by
Amicus Learning, an imprint of Amicus
P.O. Box 227
Mankato, MN 56002
www.amicuspublishing.us

Copyright © 2025 Amicus.
International copyright reserved in all countries.
No part of this book may be reproduced in any form without written permission from the publisher.

Editor: Ana Brauer
Series Designer: Kathleen Petelinsek
Book Designer and Photo Researcher: Kim Pfeffer

Library of Congress Cataloging-in-Publication Data
Names: Kammer, Gina, author.
Title: Curious about phoenix / by Gina Kammer.
Description: Mankato, MN : Amicus Learning, [2025] | Series: Curious about mythical creatures | Includes bibliographical references and index. | Audience: Ages 6–9 years | Audience: Grades 2–3 | Summary: "What powers does the phoenix have? Learn the Greek mythology about the phoenix in this question-and-answer book for elementary readers. Includes infographics, table of contents, glossary, books and websites for further research, and index"— Provided by publisher.
Identifiers: LCCN 2024017575 (print) | LCCN 2024017576 (ebook) | ISBN 9798892001007 (lib. bdg.) | ISBN 9798892001588 (paperback) | ISBN 9798892002165 (ebook)
Subjects: LCSH: Phoenix (Mythical bird)—Juvenile literature.
Classification: LCC GR830.P4 K36 2025 (print) | LCC GR830.P4 (ebook) | DDC 398.24/54—dc23/eng/20240527
LC record available at https://lccn.loc.gov/2024017575
LC ebook record available at https://lccn.loc.gov/2024017576

Photo Credits: Adobe Stock/ECrafts, cover, Spaceai, 5 (top); Alamy Stock Photo/Pictures From History, 9 (bottom); Dreamstime/Nb Art Nb, 9 (middle); Freepik/freepik, 13, kjpargeter, 13, mentas, 20–21, nitikornfreepik, 19, Pikaso, 10–11, 13, 14–15, pikepicture, 6-7; Shutterstock/AlexAnton, 16, kikujungboy CC, 13 (top); Wikimedia Commons/Boris Zvorykin (Q2613777), 9 (second from bottom), British Museum/Nic McPhee, 9 (top), Freiedrich Johann Justin Bertuch/Tsaag Valren, 18, Jpatokal, 8, Public Domain, 9 (second from bottom)

Printed in China

CHAPTER ONE 1

What is a phoenix?

A magical bird! It looks like an eagle or peacock. But it has red and gold feathers. Some say it has purple, yellow, green, and blue feathers, too. They glow brightly! When it's time, the phoenix dies in its own fire. A phoenix is born new from the ashes.

The phoenix is often associated with renewal and hope.

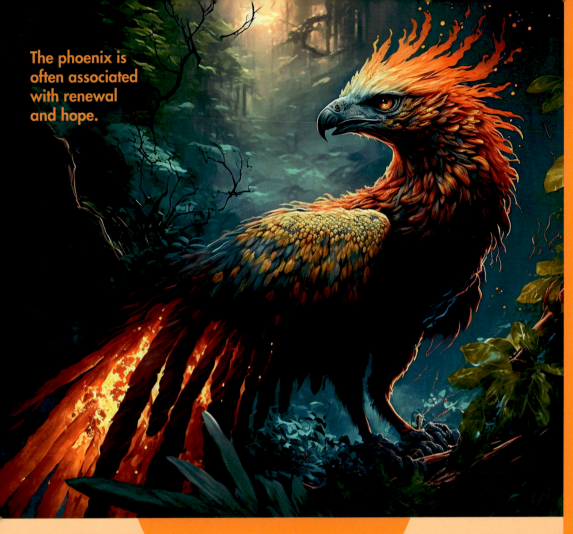

PHOENIX LEGENDS

COMPARING SIZES
How big is a phoenix?

Average human adult 6 feet (1.8 m) tall

A phoenix 3.5 ft (1.1 m) tall

An eagle 3 ft (0.9 m) tall

5

Is a phoenix real?

PHOENIX LEGENDS

In Greek and Egyptian myths, the phoenix is associated with the sun god.

Not likely. But the phoenix is a powerful, old **symbol**. It means rebirth and living forever. It is found in **myths** of Egypt, Greece, and Rome. This bird is shown in old books with real animals. But no one has **proof** that they're real.

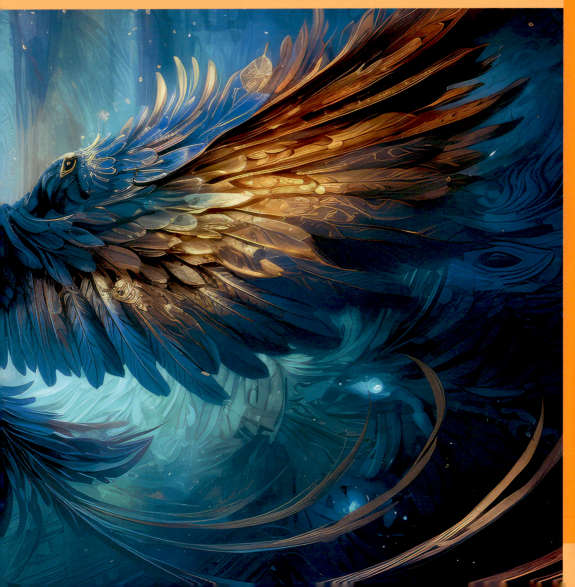

When did phoenix legends start?

The phoenix has appeared in ancient art for thousands of years.

At least 3,500 years ago. But they likely go farther back. The Greeks first wrote about the phoenix. But in Egypt, people already told stories of the Bennu. This bird was a symbol of their god. Many other cultures also have magical birds.

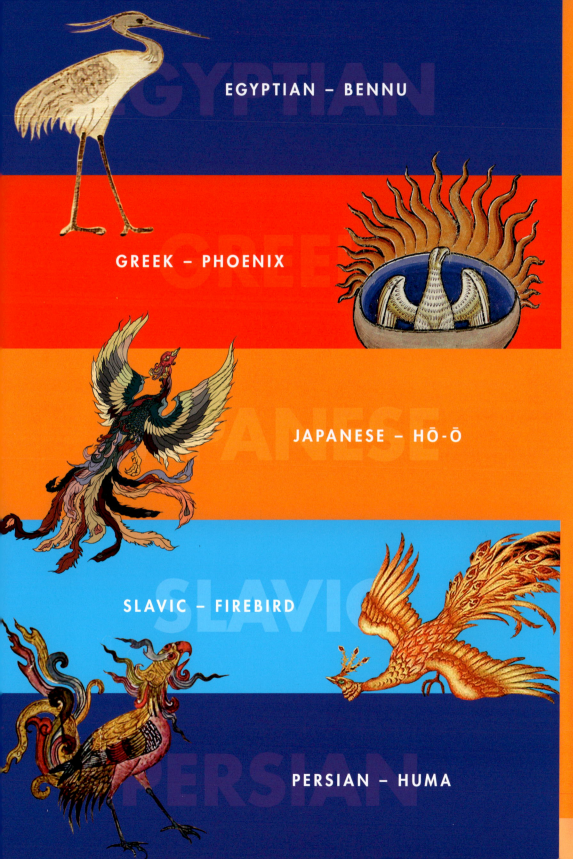

CHAPTER TWO 2

PHOENIX LIFE

How long does a phoenix live?

Depending on the story, the phoenix that is reborn could be the same phoenix that died.

PHOENIX LIFE

A long time! Most stories say a phoenix lives 500 years. In others, it's 1,000. Another story says it lives for thousands of years! But only one phoenix lives at a time. Maybe it's always the same one. Then it bursts into flame. It's born again from ashes. It starts as a worm or fully grown.

What does a phoenix eat?

Nothing! This magical creature doesn't need to eat. Instead, it smells its food! A phoenix puts spices that smell good into its nest. The scent feeds it. A phoenix also gets energy from the sun and wind. But a young phoenix may also eat drops of dew from **heaven**.

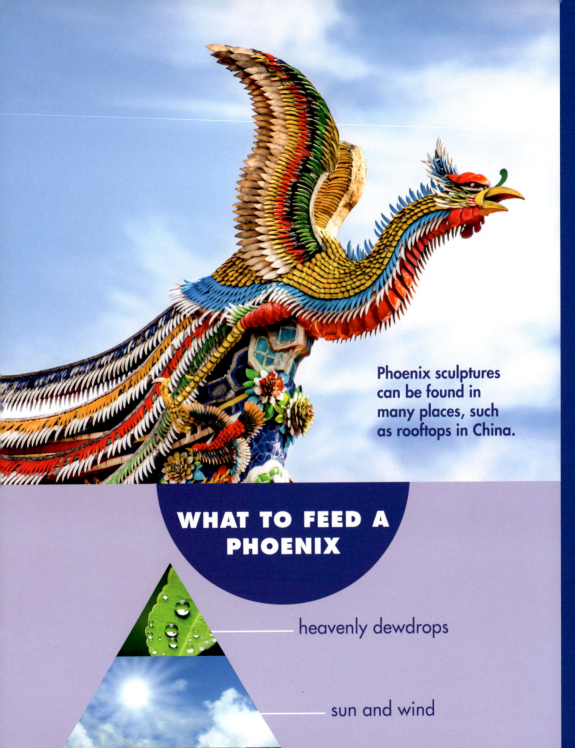

Phoenix sculptures can be found in many places, such as rooftops in China.

WHAT TO FEED A PHOENIX

- heavenly dewdrops
- sun and wind
- Arabian balsam, frankincense, cinnamon, and **myrrh**

PHOENIX LIFE

13

PHOENIX LIFE

What magic powers does a phoenix have?

Some stories say that if a phoenix is near, people can't lie.

PHOENIX LIFE

Sun power! The phoenix shines bright light. It even bursts into flame at death! It can also put the power of life into its nest. That way when it dies, a new phoenix can rise out of its ashes. Stories today also say a phoenix can heal with its tears.

15

CHAPTER THREE

Where does a phoenix live?

Ancient Greeks believed that the phoenix built its nest by the Nile River in Egypt.

In a nest! It's made of plants and spices. A phoenix wants to smell nice when it burns! The nest might be in Egypt. That's where the Greeks thought the bird lived. It could live in palm trees or near the Nile River. It will be in the sun. But it also travels to other countries.

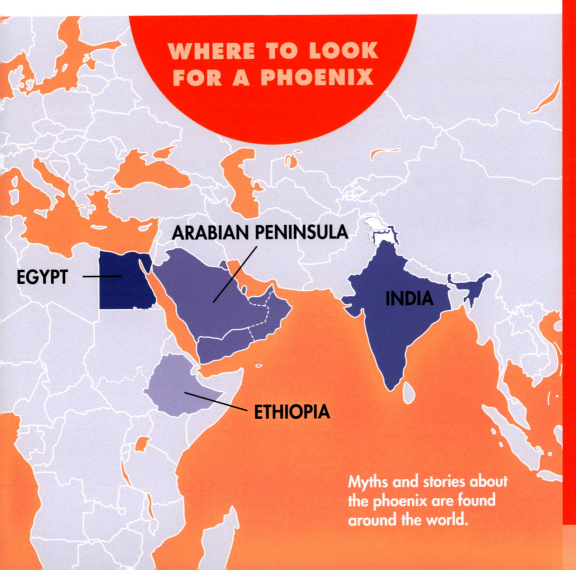

Myths and stories about the phoenix are found around the world.

FINDING PHOENIX

Has anyone seen a phoenix?

There is no proof that anyone has seen a real phoenix.

A few people say they did. An ancient Roman man wrote about a phoenix. He said it was brought to Rome. Many people saw it then. A historian wrote that people in Egypt saw a phoenix. But no one is sure they were telling the truth. They could have been other kinds of birds.

A peacock is known for its colorful feathers. People in ancient times might have thought it was a phoenix.

Can I see a phoenix?

FINDING PHOENIX

The Phoenix is a small constellation found in the southern sky.

Kind of! In early November, try looking up at the night sky. In some areas, you might be able to find a group of stars. These stars are called "Phoenix." They make a bird shape. Connect the stars like you connect dots!

FINDING PHOENIX

21

STAY CURIOUS!

ASK MORE QUESTIONS

What stories have people told about the phoenix?

What can I find out from old phoenix pictures?

Try a BIG QUESTION: Why is the phoenix a powerful symbol?

SEARCH FOR ANSWERS

Search the library catalog or the Internet.
A librarian, teacher, or parent can help you.

Using Keywords
Find the looking glass.

Keywords are the most important words in your question.

If you want to know about:

- Phoenix stories, type: PHOENIX MYTHS
- Phoenix in pictures, type: ANCIENT PHOENIX ART

LEARN MORE

FIND GOOD SOURCES

Are the sources reliable?
Some sources are better than others. An adult can help you. Here are some good, safe sources.

Books
Phoenix: Ancient Egypt's Firebird by Elizabeth Andrews, 2023.

The Phoenix by Charis Mather, 2024.

Internet Sites
Britannica Kids: Phoenix
https://kids.britannica.com/kids/article/phoenix/390048
Britannica is an encyclopedia with educational information on many topics.

Kiddle: Phoenix Facts for Kids
https://kids.kiddle.co/Phoenix_(mythology)
Kiddle is an encyclopedia for kids with facts on many topics.

Every effort has been made to ensure that these websites are appropriate for children. However, because of the nature of the Internet, it is impossible to guarantee that these sites will remain active indefinitely or that their contents will not be altered.

SHARE AND TAKE ACTION

Where can you find phoenix symbols today?
Ask an adult to help you search online or in your neighborhood.

Go to your library and find books with phoenix stories.
Read about how phoenix are shown differently in different tales.

Learn about the peacock.
How is it like a phoenix? Share what you find with friends or family.

GLOSSARY

heaven In some religions, the place people go when they die.

myrrh Dried sap from certain trees that has a strong smell.

myth An idea or story that is believed by many people but that is not true.

proof Facts or evidence that show something is true.

symbol A sign, shape, or object that stands for something else.

INDEX

birth, 4, 11
constellation, 20–21
death, 4, 15
Egypt, 6, 7, 8, 16–17, 18
food, 12–13
Greek, 8, 16, 17
lifespan, 10–11
peacock, 4, 19
symbol, 7, 8

About the Author

Gina Kammer grew up writing and illustrating her own stories. Now she teaches others to write stories at inkybookwyrm.com. She likes reading fantasy and medieval literature. She also enjoys traveling, oil painting, archery, and snuggling her grumpy bunny. She lives in Minnesota.